D0930424

Gabriel

by

George Barlow

bp

12651 Old Mill Place   Detroit, Michigan 48238

to Bobbie, my woman
Erin Ayanna, my daughter
Yvonne, my mother
Corella, my stepmother
Jo Ann & Teri, my sisters

i look upon you
& i am renewed

to George, my father
Frank, my stepfather
The strong men keep a-comin' on
The strong men git stronger.

to Mark

my little brother is a man,
a beautiful young black man

to Michael S. Harper

a black man, a friend,
a poet's poet

First Printing
First Edition
Copyright © 1974 by George Barlow
No part of this book can be copied, reproduced, or used in any
way without written permission from Broadside Press, 12651
Old Mill Place, Detroit, Michigan 48238.
Grateful acknowledgement is made for poems which appeared previously
in *Broadside Series, Heartblows: Black Veils, Intro #3, Laureate, 1970,*
and *A Galaxy of Black Writing:*
ISBN 0-910296-92-8 Cloth $5.25
ISBN 0-910296-84-7 Paper $2.00
Manufactured in U.S.A.

Table of Contents

PS
3552
A6725G3

382227

PART ONE:

CITY ROSES

All the cities are for rent.
We will rent them ourselves.

—Imamu Amiri Baraka

Cruisin' Cool

The brothers
is too much;
naturals blown-up
like blimps,
freshly cut,
rounded like moons.
Dig 'em cruisin'—
leanin' both of 'em,
six inches toward
the middle in
a new red hog,
rollin' smooth
and slow.
Look at 'em cruise;
clean as they can be,
damn neah touchin'
they leanin' so hard.
Righteously rollin'
down East 14th
takin' in the sights
through they
blue pimp shades.
The hams checkin'
and they checkin'—
clean with they
new naturals,
in the hog
cruisin' cool.
The brothers
is too much.

In Trane,
in the Groove

1.

I settle in the groove
of your soprano again;
easily, from habit.
"My Favorite Things"
& "Everytime We Say Goodbye"
comes from the box
& slows my pulse.
Things flash before me,
favorite things,
a hip history of good times.

Unwilling & unable
to move out of this groove,
I sit frozen, hypnotized,
wide open to your horn.
Wrapped in this jazz,
I go back to the block,
the Village,
to the way-out shit
we said & felt & did,
the good times we made
with our spirit & fury.

2.

The day and times we had—
our fights & loves & stolen fruit;
green peaches & belly aches;
Grand Dad & Ripple, cock & konks,
gigs & games & our sweet names:
Scooby & Shug, Punkin & Sparky,
Fritz & Wako, Dip & Bobo, Bae-bae
& Spoon, Tap & Giz, Duck & Doc,
Buggy & June Bug, Lish & Poo-poo,
Jojo & Lep, Mack & Bro, Dit-dit
& Cool, Cat Fish & Dizzy, Newt
& Cowboy, Fatso & Worm,

No-man & Pencil-man, Stewda-man
& Rabbit-man, Blue & Capone.

We were the boys, the brothers,
schemin' on the bitches, bustin'
pop bottles under street lamps;
midnight harmony & fast feet—
each of us Sam Cooke,
each of us James Brown,
all of us The Miracles & the Contours,
The Impressions & The Olympics.

Bad Man Brown & Big Boy Pete
throwin' blows on the corner again;
Stagolee & Billy gamblin'
in the dark; winos
up at the front
puking on their shadows
in front of The Rendezvous;
Hong Kong, Russian & Bullet;
sweet old brothers, sweet old wine.

People & places, the names
& the faces all easing
through my mind,
all moving with me, warm
in this groove—
Blow, Trane, blow!

3.

I turn to the music
& try to pay attention
but can't. Thinking it unheard,
missed or gone by me,
I play the side over
& over again;
a jive attempt to really listen;
you blow a few bars out
& send me off again,
back to the colors of those days;

wind & trees & sidewalk broken glass,
the summers & the snow cone truck,

the ice cream men & ice cream women,
the turf & the wars,
cool & uncool, the Esquires
& the Milk Mans in their
white coveralls & gassed heads,
bad & scared, cool & supercool,
spitting through their teeth
& sucking on tooth picks,
clowning & signifyin' in the dark:

  "Suck out my nostrils, chump."
   "Suck out Yamma's suckaaaah."
  "Who's Yamma, chump?"
   "Yamma's yo' mama, suckaaaah."

   4.

I slip & slide, trip & glide
back to the days
when we were closer to the ground,
screaming at dog fights,
girl fights, meditating
on a dead cat behind First Baptist,
the maggots in the ribs
& eye sockets teaching us
the way of death
through our sharp eyes
and willing noses.

Grasshoppers & bees
teased us then & gave us sport;
we hunted & killed them
& threw their bodies
up into the wind; we pissed
on fences, old tires, trees
& hot ash cans, giggling
at the stink.
We won trophies & races & games,
& lost marbles, grandparents,
eyes & limbs—Earl's right arm,
Sherman & Lavaughn an eye apiece.

5.

Blow, Trane! Blow that breeze
through my knee-patched jeans
& my talking tennis shoes.

Blow that wind & rain
over me & the boys,
it feels good.

Blow me away, for secretly
locking Sam's dog, Frankie,
in the garage & peein'

all over him
to pay him back
for leaning against my leg

& peein' all over
my new Buster Browns
while I snoozed in the sun—

Blow, Trane!
Gone on melody, lost in jazz,
I go back & back & back

to & through those days
& spin in their sweetness.
Go 'head, Trane!

"My Favorite Things"
f'days—dig it!
Trippin' back in Trane.

The music is the groove:
I do it & feel it
& play it all over again.

for Willie, one of the boys

10

Mellowness & Flight

ever heard Bird
flap his wings

ever heard him
play Lover Man
Laura
Just Friends

ever taken
his mellowness in
& felt

like
you were
flying
with him

shining like him

a bright blackbird
slicing blue sky

sweetly & freely

ever heard Bird
flap his wings

for Charlie Parker

Mingus Speaks:
Found Poems

1.

the soloists
at Birdland

had to wait for
Parker's next record

to find out
what to play

           what
will they do now

        2.

     hey dig
Bird ain't dead
he's hiding out
somewhere

& he'll be back
with some new shit

that will scare
everyone to death

                                    for Bird

Bird

I heard that Bird
was shootin' up once
with two young dudes
who dug him so much—
cause he was Bird,
baddest cat on earth—
that they let
him fix first.
Heard that Bird,
diggin' their
little brotherness
& love
fixed himself
& accidently
smashed their smack
on the floor—
dig it!
Bird.
     Sweetest cat
that ever lived.

            for Charlie "Yardbird" Parker

12

Out of It

(Ain't no air up there, baby!)

Sniffing quickly,
zooming his nostrils wide,
he snorts goofer dust
from a fingernail file;
zips it into his skull
& shuts his eyes
while it melts
down his limbs
& tingles him—
ass, finger tips, knees, toes.

Stoned, froze,
turned around,
he sings his song:

"I'm high,
flyin' high in the sky—
high up
& hip—
              dig it!
I fly & trip.
High. High. High.
Skyin', baby—
forever high—
                        dig it!
I'm what's happenin'.
Shiiiiiiiiiiiit!
Everything is everything.
I can fly high—
hey man—
like higher than yesterday.
Up, up & away—
                        dig it!
High & Black,
stoned & hip,
he tries to fly up
from the shit on the ground—
gestapo cops in helicopters,
brothers dead & dying,

13

bricks & bullets flying,
mothers screaming/crying.
High.
High up
the hip brother trips—
hard & high,
way up on that cloud
where he thinks
he can breathe.

City Roses
(Want some fun, baby?)

Blooming patiently
in every corner
of this nervous garden,
these roses spread
their petals
for bumblebees
to come in
and leave their pollen;
green, folded,
tucked away for safety
in half hidden blossoms.
A blackbird sings blues
from the juke box
in a hot links joint nearby.
Scooby cruises
through his garden
and whispers to a rose:
"Turn a lotta sunshine, baby!
Take in plenty pollen,
sweet-fine-thang!"

Swashbuckler

It's dark at last
& a long chrome vessel
cruises conspicuously
up & down
this jittery red light sea.

The pilot, a plump gull,
stares silently
at a mermaid
he has selected
from the spectrum.

Smooth, bronze, sparkling,
she waits
singular
in a cove for
cash & company.

Passing slowly, the grey
swashbuckler becomes captain
of a pirate ship.
In a moment
he'll buy some plunder.

He'll
bring the wench on board
& take her
below.
It's dark at last.

Kareem Abdul-Jabbar

last night
i saw
the brother jump
high enough to
go into orbit

ZOOOOOOOOOOM!

saw him
stretch like a rubber band
& stuff his new name
down that
sportscaster's white throat

THOOOOOOOOOOM!

through the hoop—

"The shot is gooooooood!
Two points for
Abduuuuuuuuuuuul-Jabbaaaaaaaaaaar!"

saw him
grip the ball
like it was the moon
& fade-away
a tidal wave
into wilt's chest

SWISH!

(wilt stunned—
damn near got washed
all the way back up
to his million dollar crib
on his own million dollar hill)

saw him
shoot mojo juju
voodoo & hoodoo
hooks

ZIP! ZIP! ZIP! ZIP!

saw him
draw fouls
from corny grey boys
who couldn't
get out of the way

BAM! BAM!

"Jabbar at the free throw line—
Will shoot two."

POW! POWER!

saw him
bop & stride
up & down the court
like he owned it

    jabbar—
    abdul-jabbar

      dig it!

kareem abdul-jabbar!

Sly

Everybody is a star—
I can feel it
When you shine on me. . . .

      Stone
out of your mind,
crazier than
the craziest sonuvagun,
totally beautiful,
you are
the music you make.

      Squares & fools
discuss your madness,
scratch their block heads
in bafflement,
& strain to comprehend
you & your family.

      Unable
to locate you on their
grid, they assume
you've blown your way
out into insanity.
They don't know!
      Clean

as you can be,
funkier than ever,
wholly soulful,
you've stepped off
the grid
out onto a star.

Stay
out there, mah man.
you 'bout the baddest
thang in the sky.

for Sly Stone

The Justifiable Hunt

I saw him move into the jungle
secretly out in the open,
smiling, cocksure

the safari would go well.
With hard hat, map
& a change of black shirts

he tracks down panthers
& puts notches on his gun
(twenty-eight to date).

When he returns to civilization
he will receive blessings
& a bonus check for bravery

because the public
won't know that the
fierce black cats he hunts

are strictly defensive animals.
And he won't tell,
& let his long hours of

Travel & planning be wasted.
He says the hunt must continue.
And it does.

Reverend Jesse in Gary
(Repeat after me, brothers & sisters!)

I AM SOMEBODY!
I AM SOMEBODY!
I AM SOMEBODY!
I MIGHT BE UNEDUCATED,
BUT I AM SOMEBODY!
I MIGHT BE ON WELFARE,
BUT I AM SOMEBODY!
I AM SOMEBODY!
I AM SOMEBODY!

The groove is made
& we echo
our total belief
in what we repeat:
I AM SOMEBODY!
I AM SOMEBODY!

We send our groove up.
The walls & roof
of this great gym
could explode or melt away;
we're so black
so mighty, SOMEBODY.

Revivified, energized,
turned-on to ourselves,
we'll spill into
the mills in the morning
still spinning in the groove
of this evening.

I AM SOMEBODY!
I AM SOMEBODY!
I AM SOMEBODY!

Preach, Reverend Jesse!

19

Flowers at
the Jackson Funeral Home
(Daddy? Sugardaddy? You really dead?)

Standing silently
about eight safe feet
from the casket,
these five
night-blooming cereuses
fix their eyes
on the slim
stuffed pimp
whose heart
ruptured monday.
Their collective
fragrance
is sweeter than roses
& more expensive.
Their bright vines
cling & squeeze
their blossoms up
blending them nicely
with the other
flowers about.
Half-paniced
being here,
too bothered
to stay away, each
fine night flower
is petrified
& waits numbly
for the resting figure
to suddenly awake
& glance over
with quick frozen eyes
which shout:
"Trick, Bitch! Trick!"

PART TWO: UNCLE JESSE

I am telling you this:
history is your own heartbeat.

—Michael S. Harper

George Wylder Barlow, Jr.

            i used to didn't
            dig my name too much

            george

                    shiiiiiiiiiiiiit

            that ain't no name
            for nobody

                        nobody black

            my daddy
            didn't give me no slack

            but now
            it don't seem so bad

                        not so bad

            at all
            george

                    shiiiiiiiiiiiiit

            i got me a

                        baaaaaaaaaaaaaad

            aaaaaaaaaaaaaaased

                        name

                                for George Jackson

Reality Is a Broken Nose
(Oh brother, I'm sorry . . . . is it, is it broken?)

            This ain't real.
            The four anesthetic needles
            that stick our from my nostrils,
            the veins in my wet eyes,
            the clotting in my mustache,
            the odd Karate crook

22

in my local, far away nose,
make me a shrunken head
or something
to frighten children with.

Gauze, alcohol.
Tear glands & ducts
flood these cheeks;
nerves & eyebrows, tilted back
on this bed,
twitch under the light
& sterile machinery above.
This ain't happening.

As skilled fingers lean in
to crunch cartilage, bone
& nasal pride back into place,
I want to scream at
the twist of this thing:
my fellow Karateka & I
sparring, polishing our techniques,
immunizing ourselves against
those who would break our bones.
I can't take
the antiseptic taste in my mouth;
the medical workings upon me;
this ain't real.

Mammy

She was Pearl
with the cushion cocoa arms
to cradle him in old songs,
unforgotten lore,
to the rhythm of tiny
cherry cheeked pumpings
at the nipples
of her dark perfect bosom.
Nestle in tightly,
the small blond skull

took music and
the nourishment in.

She was Pearl
who died
in his sixth year
leaving him with
the old songs,
unforgotten lore,
the music and the
nourishment.
Her death,
whispered to him by
the other woman
with blond hair like his,
made him cry
the rest of his life.

for John Peter

Sweet Diane

I see that you're a poetry lover, sweet Diane,
little Fifth Grade diamond girl,
lonely little student of mine.
You say that you don't like P.E.,
that you'd rather "make poems"—
me too, baby, me too.

So we sit here on a frozen December bench,
make frosty conversation,
and watch a crucial kickball game.
It's cold out here—
too cold for these little *chilums*.

You say your best friend was offed?
A teen-age boy cracked her head
with a big rock? (Damn!)
And she died in Brookside Hospital on Halloween?
Did this really happen,

or is it the glitter
of your sweet Fifth Grade imagination?

Wish I could believe you made it up.
But I can't.
It's real, baby,
too real for all of us.

What did you do with your tears?
Did you make a poem, sweet Diane?
All this cold, that big rock,
And your dead girlfriend
are the reflections of our world.
Why don't you shine back on them
with a poem this afternoon?
Why don't you save us
with a poem, sweet Diane?

for Diane Ramirez

The Tears, the Honeydew

It's a terrible & beautiful
song you sing; bitter
like tears, sweet
like honeydew.

Your stomach is a smooth
brown melody ready
to issue its goodness
after nine months on the vine.

Yesterday swift
surgical hands slipped
the batholin cist away
& cleared the path
for dawn-fruit & placenta.
Perfection was yours
& you rehearsed a lullaby.

Today began with
uterine flood tides

& pelvic earthquakes
that made you sing
louder & stronger than
you've ever sung before.

It's a terrible & beautiful
song you sing; bitter
like tears, sweet
like honeydew.

It's time.
Etherized, popped up,
& gently spread,
you're a vaginal vine
on a giant trellis
contorting beneath
an electric sun
that shines hotly on
the twitching ripe melon.
And you sing, agonized.

Suddenly a daughter
is where wish & dream were.
But death has come;
a hemophilic nightmare;
a bright red stream
unforeseen.

You've sung your
last song
& your child is singing
her first—
a born soloist
singing to her father.

It's a terrible & beautiful
song you sing; bitter
like tears, sweet
like honeydew.

for George Barlow, Sr.,
on the death of Ethel &
the birth of Teri Lynn

In the Faculty Room
at an Elementary School
in California

Waistlines & yogurt chatter in a hen's voice,
sugarless tongues going berserk at noon,
a wrinkled Fourth Grade overseer is
burning the air with garlic & a wild
Halloween party over the weekend,
a penny for the old girl
Who went as Cinderella.

I am the only one her
The cottage cheese smiles &
the saccharine stares tell me
how weird I am—
a Black ghost teaching in Room 20
on this nice October day,
how appropriate, how novel.

Etiquette on Field Trip,
a Narrative Poem

While standing in front of
the panther cage
at San Francisco Zoo today,

little black third grade Moses
suddenly asked big white
teacher Mr. O'Pharaoh:

"What did dat cat do
t'git hisself locked up
like dat, teachah?"

And big white Mr. O'Pharaoh
answered: "Eat your popcorn,
Moses."

27

And little black Moses
continued: "But how did. . . ."
But big Mr. O'Pharaoh interrupted:

"Don't talk with
your mouth full, son,
let's go see the parrots."

Early to School
("Learn it to the younguns")

Those tiny black faces,
breakfastless & ashy
with dried tears,
glide cooly across
the little tadpole bridge
on their way to Verde School
& pay no mind to
the black & white sow
sitting by the field,
over to the right,
staring strangely—
searching perhaps
for dynamite or
a nine-year-old machine-gunner.
They keep coming—
ham & bacon on their minds—
the sow's eyes on their bodies.
Here come the younguns!
Here come the younguns!
Here come the younguns!

Number Eight Apollo

Figure-eighting
around moon and earth,
doing the dance of the bees,

sending pictures and prayers
back for publication,
these three lunar men do their
Buck Rogers gallantly.
Nobody would want to spoil
a perfect figure eight.

Apollo Eleven

the metallic housefly
paused on green cheese
is puking up two million
green gunky chunks
part of washington's nose
lincoln's mole/wart
franklin's razor lips
& two pink
moon men
are floating tracks
on the old dusty face
in front of
an old black sister
down in the delta
focusing
on the moon

American Empire

the draft
from the great
beating wings
of the bald eagle—
its greenish
blood-stained
feathers oily
& spread everywhere—
takes the young man

up into its talons
to be carried/ripped off
& set down
in the north
or south or east
or west
to guard what
the sun never sets on

for Jug, infantryman

Tract

It's the Fifth of July!

Thunder. Lightning. Rain.
The ritual is postponedd:
the Lawd done put it off a day.
(And I can dig it!)

So these half-tanned citizens
have come out tonight
to cheer & thrill
at fake bombs bursting in air.

And they are bored.

I've come to watch them
I'm high on them
& I trip on them,
as they surely trip on me,
as I'm black, as there is
nothing else for them to do.

Here is a bald, T-shirted man
his neck & cheeks reddening
as he blurts to his family
& all in ear-shot:
"Christ! This thing is moving
too slow—they should
shoot the damn things faster!"
(And I can dig it!)

They should
shoot the damn things
at the crowd—
that would be hip.

Or an even better trip,
tie one of these Iowa Citizans
(that darker one over there)
to one of these city park trees
& burn him—
accuse him of rape or something—
geld him, carve on him,
& set fire to him.

Real fireworks is their due.
(Dig it!)
They should revisit
the workings of fire
on flesh.

These citizens came out
after a year & a day of waiting
to receive their communion.
And they should
receive it,
take it in—
not some jive 1776 abstraction,
but the real thing.

Their nostrils & lungs
should be filled
with the smoke
of the real past.
They should be
sickened to death, not bored.
It's their right.

It's the Fifth of July!

Last Night
I Dreamt of Mushrooms

they're finally
leaving earth
& coming back again

arching
all over the world

the slender menaces
the thermal fingers
are blotting the sky out

mushrooming
from ultimate fireworks
heralded by
the last siren
the noon whistle gone berserk

all the thinking
talking
crying/writing/singing
means nothing now

this is
the last mistake

there will be no more

here are blacks
whites/old people/children
midgets & giants
burrowing numbly
into their shelters
to die

this is
the last nightmare

there will be no more

the mushrooms
are sprouting
mindlessly
totally
finally

Nigger

An experiment
gone out of control.
Kissed by Hysteria
in a bad twentieth century dream,
the pale scientists speak. . . .
The savages are running
wild in the streets;
creating & multiplying like hell.
The horror! The horror!

We have made monsters
goddamn our mad souls.
Our hollow cores cry out—
Exterminate the brutes!
Exterminate the brutes!
Exterminate the brutes!

8 Ball

Smooth round black,
with a little white paint
on his face
they call him 8 Ball
& hate him.

He is involved
to the hilt
& not at all;
his views aren't
asked of him,
but he has some.

Saved for last,
he is the most important
shot of all.
And when hit too hard
by the stick
he flies flaming off the table
& into the streets.

Cab

(after hearing that Cab Calloway hipped-up the National Anthem once upon a time & was subsequently banned from public broadcasts for a while)

It was you, Cab,
                    who
            brought life
                    to
            THE BIG SONG,
                        which was
                cotton fields
            & death.

You,
        drew sweetness
    from cane
                    made bitter by
    rum, slave trade,
                & bleeding harvest.

Minstrel & myth,
                        you
    lulled ole massah with
            "Daddy Dear"
                            sweetly

& he loved you.
But now
            you've
    put a pulse
                where
        a star-spangled secret was;
    the rhythm
                is changed
& he
        hates you for it.

Bangladesh Blues

you've died
many times
before

but never
ever
like this

swollen with loss
swollen with love
swollen with anger

you move
slowly
on the tv news

here is one
here is another
here are ten more

the count is up
three million
& rising

thin black
bodies
in your front yard

we watch you cry
& count them
& cover them with earth

the wolf pack is gone
& you are free
Joy! Joy! Bangla!

but victory here
is a body count
a plum in your throat

an old handkerchief
at your cheeks
& eyes

for Sheikh Mujib

Jolson

fake skin
& fake lips

brought you
good fortune

we see no kinship
in your face

you've sung
an evil song

about our mother
count jolson

& they
love you for it

Roots

(They say if a South Carolina Geeche woman want you,
ain't nothin' you can do!)

Ole mean Jimmie
ain't so mean no mo'—
ain't whupped his ole lady
in a week or so—
used to slap the girl
and leave her cryin';
now he in bed
slowly dyin'.

Went upside her head
too many times, ole Jim,
and now she done
worked roots on him.
They say he won't
last till Sunday
cause she got a roach
growin' in his belly.

for Bennie Arkwright

To a Sister
Whose Naturally Straight
Hair Gives Her the Blues

Hey baby,
don't be blue
cause you think
we don't love you
cause you ain't got no
big bushy Afro
like you think
you suppose to.

Don't be sad,
sweet thang,
cause yo' hair
don't seem to fit
into this here new pride
we ridin'
to the new world on.

Hop on board, sugar mama,
with yo' bad natural self!

for Boo

Corkscrew

Yesterday
        I'm
laying-up in the crib
            digging
Lew Rawls blow
                "Strange Fruit"

& Scotty
        my main man
    dropped by.

He'd copped
     some Chianti—
grapes for
          our kinship—
     dig it!
Needed a corkscrew.
                    Piss!
I broke downstairs
          to cop one
from my
     grey neighbors,
knowing they'd have one.

          As I descended
I tried
     to remember
where I'd read about
     Charlie & Ann
using corkscrews
          on brothers
     at lynchings,
  & wondered if
the one I was after
          had ever
pulled out flesh
          of my flesh.
I copped it,
          dug
     how old it was
& damn near
     got mad.

Romance Is a Butterfly,
White Folks & Dust

From a groove
in my old couch
I dig on
the worn cellulose
of Hollywood's jive west:

a pinto, gunfire, a fence post;
empty passion
& minstrelsy
flickering on the tube.

Here in the purity
of violins & frontier dust
are sexless grey
cowboys & cowgirls
bullshitting in the sun.

And at their feet—

caught in the mud
& steer shit
caught on their boots—

is the cattle king's
nigger maid, Vashti,

a frail little
buck-eyed butterfly
who flutters
in & out of focus
humming to herself,

filling the screen sometime,
flapping her wings
in mystic innocence.

In this old west
that never was
the pure pioneers
piss on their butterfly

& let her
fuss over them

while they trip
on empire,
tangle their privates
in barbed wire romance,
& rip each other off.

I could dig
jumping these eunuchs

    & gunning them down
    & liberating
    the butterfly

but they're only
phantoms
on the late show;

    a goddamned grey nightmare;
    a funkyassed dream.

for Butterfly McQueen

Blood/Line

this young
             white
bank teller

tells me
his last name is
the same as
             mine

that there aren't
many of us
             around

what's he telling
me
       this shit for

we ain't
          related

Uncle Jesse

My cousin Tracy
your nephew
tells me that
a Louisiana white man
shouted some real ugly shit
at my aunts Betsy and Sandie Mae
your sisters
from a slow-moving train
and that
you snatched this white man
from that train and nearly
beat him to death
and that
from a high white bench

you were sentenced to life
and that
you were only seventeen.

Tracy tells me that our family
under the lead of Kit Monroe
your daddy
worked and worked and worked
and schemed and kissed
and managed to get you out
after one eternal year
so you could finish high school
eat gumbo
and live like a human being
and things like that.

I understand the beautiful
state of Louisiana told you
to leave her bosom
and never return—
an order which, if disobeyed,
could cost you your FREEDOM.

Tracy tells me that
the evil you whipped
stayed on the operating table
for thirty-six hours
before the doctors agreed
that he would
live on and on and on.

PART THREE:
LOVE SONG

I will build you a castle with a tower so high
That it reaches the moon.

I'll gather melodies from birdies that fly
And compose you a tune.

Give you lovin' warm as mama's oven—
If that don't do, then I'll try something new.

—Smokey Robinson

Oakland: Our First Home

The creek
runs under our street
past the Panther office
& the Coliseum.
Its music comes
up two stories;
the sweet sonata,
the cricket concerto
of our first bed.

Moments ago we
grooved into each other
& moved through
a love dance—
ultimate union—
a spirit, a love supreme.

Now we lie shining,
harmoniously fatigued;
music of the crickets
& frogs & water.
And we almost forget
about the
nightsticks & howls.

for Bobbie

Touch

If, in my half-sleep,
I squeeze you
a little too hard,
or spoil
the pinned plan
of your hair,
or lock
one of your bronze flanks

between my knees
in the wee hours
of a freezing Iowa night,
it's because
I'm glad that
you're my woman,
& because
I dig sharing
warm darkness
with you.
Why else
would I do this?

The Grooming

love is touch
touch is love

with one hand
he gently holds
his son's tiny head—

an almond
in a rough
human palm—

with the other
he passes a comb
through the shiny

young bush
that easily gives way
to this sunday morning grooming

in a moment
he'll slowly twirl
his little likeness

hunt for specks of lint
on the minature suit
& dust off the tiny loafers

then he'll smile
at the little dude
request a sunday morning hug

& almost burst
as he watches him
coolly strut

into the living room
with his shimmering head
cocked to one side

& one hand softly jingling
change in his pocket
like someone else does

for Frank & Mark Fisher

Meditation before the Rain

In this hour
it is warm—
things are as they should be.
Huge grey & black thunderclouds
move overhead
& bump each other softly.
Music in the sky.

Children hustle about
on the brown grass
beneath my porch
in drunken afternoon play.
Whole insect nations
have vanished
with the sun.

Lightning flashes pink
behind muffled timpani clouds.
I smell the rain coming,

watch the ground darken
under tiny speeding feet,
feel moist & alive, & know
I am where I should be.

*for **Tony Colby***

Love Song

you really
pissed me off
this morning

no—
all day long!

with all that
bullshit
you was putting down

& all that
mute walking around

not speaking
like
i wasn't there

& now
you come floating
up behind me

to cling
like a kitten
or a ladybug

knowing i won't
move
or sling you off

knowing i'll take you
back in

She Complains

She complains
that I never tell her
I love her,
that I'm holding back;
being cool.
Poets know how to
say these things
in beautiful ways
that cuddle
their loved ones, she mumbles.
I lie mute, half-listening,
holding her close to me;
feeling her lips
tease my shoulder;
her precious breath
complaining.

Lust As Distraction:
An Unwritten Poem

how can i
write
when she
keeps tipping
into this room

innocently
filling it
each time
with those
two swollen melons

those smooth
chocolate shoulders

& that
sweet new curve
to her belly

again
i lay
will & pen
before my pregnant
dahomey queen

4 1/2 Months: Halfway Song
(Hey, Baby! What you know good?)

Cuddled in the dark,
we place our hands
on the sturdy brown bulb
to feel
the life thumps
of what we've made
with our love.
I tell her
it's a message;
my African son
drumming on the wall.
She tells me
it's my African daughter
dancing to the rhythm
of her own fetal heartbeat.
We agree that
love is a black baby
growing in our hearts.

Gas

My woman says it's gas
in my daughter's belly
that makes her flash
a quick smile
from time to time.
I say it's magic & love.

Deranged from no sleep,
bright images of an easy birth
still oozing in & out of my head,
I sit rocking my firstborn;
a tiny rosebud
only eight days old.

From the stereo grooves
in a jam on the box,
Cannonball cuddles her
softly in jazz,
in the warm wings of birdland:
alto lullaby, alto love.

Soulfully he blows
"Two Sleepy People"
& my dawn eyes stop burning
as the budding little flower
smiles quickly in her sleep.

It can't be gas.
It has to be magic—
Cannonball & the sweet horn,
love & her old man's
rocking heartbeat—
that makes her bloom.

for Erin Ayanna

50

PART FOUR:
GABRIEL

Throughout history, the powers of single black men flash here and there like falling stars, and die sometimes before the world has rightly gauged their brightness.

—W.E.B. DuBois

Gabriel

*From what he said to me, he seemed to have
made up his mind to die, and to have re-
solved to say but little on the subject of the
conspiracy.*

—James Monroe

I

THE TRUMPETER

He is Gabriel;
black man & slave;
blacksmith/rebel leader;
Thom Prosser's nigger;
black man, armed & thinking,
blending with the landscape,
plotting in the swamp.

He is Gabriel;
big black preacher man;
conspirator & warrior;
Samson in Virginia,
who won't apologize
in the end,
who'll be mute
like Miles
in the end—
black & beautiful
in the end.

He is Gabriel,
who blows walls down;
fighter of thunder & lightning;
Shango in Virginia,
betrayed by monkeys & rain;
black man & slave,
who carries a big stick.

He is Gabriel;
history & myth;
blood & guts & change;
legend & husband;

brother & black man.
                    Gabriel.
Gabriel is a black man.

II

THE WILL & THE SWAN

In the slave quarters
& the tobacco fields,
under pine branches

& hardwood leaves,
in the marsh grass
of the swamp,

the kitchens,
stables & smokehouses
of the plantations,

the rebels
dream of the blow
on Richmond,

Monroe, Jefferson
& the country.
Silently,

through the seasons,
they burrow into
the fertile underground

& ready themselves.
In the perfect light
of their own darkness,

the private gleam
of their own
golden will,

they watch their leader
become
a great black swan,

& under his wing
they patiently, soulfully
let the plot ferment.

III

SPIRIT IN THE DARK

*They that walked in darkness sang songs in
the olden days—Sorrow Songs—for they
were weary at heart.*

—W.E.B. DuBois

Here is the spirit in the dark
Here is the spirit in the dark
Here is the spirit in the dark

One heart, one voice,
one purpose: Black angels
singing in a shack
near Richmond; blowing
the Sorrow Songs
that are hope & renewal.

Hear it in the dark
Here is the spirit in the dark

One people, one dream,
one collective beauty
gathered in secret to feel
the spirit in the dark:
rhythm, harmony, melody:
the seeds of soul:
Aretha, Mahalia, Nina.

See it in the dark
Touch it, hear it, feel it in the dark

Under an old roof that leaks
& an old system
that won't let them breathe,
they blow their urgency,
rebirth & survival, sweetly
like wind through reeds & treetops.

Get it in the dark
Gotta get the spirit in the dark

In the guts of slavery,
in the horror of the times,

54

they sing the songs
loudly & softly,
feeling the spirit in the dark;
planting the seeds:
B.B., Otis, Sam.

Hear it in the dark
I know you hear the spirit in the dark

They're ready in the dark
'cause they've got the feeling;
Africans in the dark; strong
in the spirit in the dark;
Trane in the dark;
Billie, Diz, & Bird in the dark;
feel them in the spirit,
feel them in the dark.

Seed, ancestors, angels in the dark;
all feeling, all spirit in the dark;
all powerful in the spirit;
heart, soul & love in the dark;
freedom in the spirit;
Gabriel in the dark;
the Trumpeter in the spirit in the dark.

Here is the spirit
Here is the dark
Here is the spirit in the dark

IV

COMING & GOING:
GABRIEL'S SONG

Fixing my eyes downward,
moving slow & easy
to go unnoticed,
I enter Richmond
for the twentieth time.

I squint kindly
at the masters' & mistresses'
Sunday dress
as it brightens up the storefronts—

every porch, every door, every window
has a place in my mind.
Smiling at these folks,
bowing my head
as they pass,
I note the sidewalk;
how it's gotten
hard & rough & dusty
under their evil feet.

Gotta get so I
can call up
every board ,every nail,
every footprint
in my mind; gotta be ready
to call every splinter.

Come next Saturday evening,
Lord willing,
we're coming in to open up
all these doors & windows
& all these big white bellies.
We're gonna stand up tall
& sing up to heaven
when we take this town.

V

THE RAINBOW

Here
is America's killing;
death by knife & fire;
& in the rainbow
are the Methodists,
the Quakers,
some poor whites,
some Frenchmen,
the Catawba Indians,
& the Blacks
in brown, tan,
jet, high yeller—
the various colors

of a conspiracy
to survive.

        Blending
perfectly & desperately,
they know
that in this last blaze
only monsters will die.

        Here
is America's killing:
survivors will be
radiant, guiltless,
human.

VI

WHITE BLUES:
THE MASTER'S SONG

Dawn again
& no sleep;
jumping & sweating
where sweet dreams
should be.
Red-eyed & trembling,
he sits on the back porch,
watches the sun
sneak up
over the tobacco rows
& thinks about
the easy, lazy world
that suckled him—
the plump black Mammy
whose lap & songs
sent him off each night,
the white pony
his daddy bought,
& old Josh
who'd dance,
tell him stories
& tickle him.

He sits

digging his nails
into the arm
of an ancient white rocker
wondering where
that world went,
wondering what happened
to the blacks—
"No good niggahs,
ungrateful black devils,
what the hell happened to 'em?
Ain't like they used to be!"

Lately he's felt
something brewing
right here
in Henrico County—
insurrection maybe—
but that's silly,
he thinks,
just silly fretting.

In the dawn shadows
he can barely make out
the figure
of his blacksmith, Gabriel,
scratching a strange rhythm
on the whetstone:
putting a fine edge
on the cook's butcher knife.
Silly fretting.
This will be
a good day;
a hog up for slaughter;
plenty for all,
like always.

VII

HISTORY
IS THUNDER & RAIN

Wind, rain,
cracks in the sky:
a strange storm

has come to stop
the march;

high water
splashing from hell;
the Brook Swamp bridge
washed out—

Gabriel
& one thousand armed blacks
can't cross
into Richmond.

Shocked, hunched
& glazed,
they stand soaked
in the impotence
of this strange rain.

Those months
of building, whetting,
oiling the secret arsenal
have turned to mud
under their feet.

Across the flood
the militia waits;
howling
in the freak Virginia night;
signalled by Mosby Sheppard

whose two black sheep,
Tom & Pharoah,
lost their way
into history, thunder & rain,
a plot to insurrect.

VIII

THE FERRETS

The ferrets are out!
The ferrets are out!

Run away, run away

The ferrets are out

covering the county
Hide & keep quiet
white phantoms of inquisition

Run away, run away

covering the countryside

Damn 'em, Damn 'em

howling & hunting
Quiet, keep quiet

through mud & woods
through kitchens & fields
tracking blacks
howling & hunting

The ferrets are out!
The ferrets are out!

to purge & ferret

Run, Gabe, run

shoot & kill

Steal away, brother, steal away

question & question

Run away, run away

kill & kill

Sail away, Gabriel, sail away

The ferrets are out!
The ferrets are out!

"Where is Gabriel?"

Run, run

"His bitch? His brother?"

Sail, Gabe, sail

"Get the blacksmith!"

Can't sail, can't sail

60

"Find him!"

     Can't hide

"Dig the coon out!"

     Can't run anymore

"Get him! Get him!"

     They'll get me but I'm a man

"Take him alive. He must talk!"

     Ain't saying a mumblin' word

"Get the nigger, make him talk!"

     I can die

"He's got to tell us how he did it!"

     I'm Gabriel
     I'm a black man
     I ain't afraid

IX

LIFE AND DEATH:
THE BITCH'S BREW
THE READINESS IS ALL

He is death
in life
& life in death
in the dim pregnancy

of these eleven days
in the hold
of the schooner *Mary*
in Norfolk harbor;

waiting for posse,
trial & rope;
waiting to be born
into martyrdom;

waiting for white Justice—
a blind bitch—

to deliver him, stillborn,
into her bleeding history;

a tapestry of
swollen middle passage blacks
drowned in a net
& gelded bucks in poplar trees.

Having tossed bayonet & bludgeon—
his only arms—
overboard,
he contemplates providence,

revisits that stormy night,
& worries about his wife, Nanny,
his lieutenant, Jack Bowler,
his two brothers, Solomon & Martin.

Secretly he tightens his resolve
to say nothing of them
in the end;
to be mute in the end.

Hearing no sounds
but the music
of his own heartbeat
& breathing,

he privately,
fearlessly prepares
for the stages of his stillbirth:
mock trial, mob, scaffold.

How many times
can the bitch kill him,
swing the trap open
& break his neck?

She will hear
no confession, see no fear,
& scream out,
unsatisfied.

X

OCTOBER, 1800:
A SON IN THE CONTINUUM

Behold, a son!

The product of our love:
a worker
born into the slavery
of Southampton,
born sturdy & black
on this 2nd day of the month.

Behold, a cosmic birth!

We welcome this newborn
& note his timing;
Gabriel's conviction
is tomorrow—on the 7th
he will hang.

Behold, a manchild!

A newborn worker
of the soil; a black boy
in the tidewater landscape:
a son in the continuum:
Africa in Virginia,
manchild in Southampton,
Gabriel in the manchild.

Behold, a gift!

Our own substance:
black flesh, black bone,
black fiber & liquids—
a newborn warrior—
our son,
Nat! Nat Turner!